Praise for Elizabeth Vignali's **House of the Silverfish**

In Elizabeth Vignali's *House of the Silverfish*, stars "strum out" above people frying potatoes for dinner. The human heart is green like a stem. The human heart is a whale's heart—like layers of parchment—filleted open. What strikes me about this collection is its dissonance, how Vignali, an expert at cinematographic image, is also critical of the poetic impulse to catalogue: "Audubon killed thousands of birds in an effort to capture their images." I have never read a more compassionate speaker, or work more concerned with the connectedness between complicity and love.

—Taneum Bambrick, author of *Vantage* and *Reservoir*

"There will always be something / to pay for, there will always be something to love," Elizabeth Vignali writes in a poem called "Mortgage," and that tension thrums throughout this collection. Vignali's lines seek language for our obligations and our hungers, our needs and our wants. This book is about motherhood, about marriage, about the varied ways we break and mend—and there's beauty in all of it. A moment late in the collection offers this: "I read somewhere that because electrons / have a negative charge / we can never actually touch anything," but these poems certainly touch their readers, reaching out with unflinching tenderness.

—Amorak Huey, author of *Boom Box*, *Ha Ha Ha Thump*, and *Poetry: A Writer's Guide and Anthology*

What does it mean to occupy a body, a house, a marriage? Or, perhaps more to the point: What might it mean to occupy the identity of woman, homeowner, wife? These are no easy shoes to walk in, especially when you "struggle with knowing / how to be a person at all." But in Elizabeth Vignali's *House of the Silverfish,* we have gods, myths, and bird after bird to guide our steps forward, even as those steps falter. Though she tells us that "when all else fails, know how to mourn," it seems in these poems that the answer too might be to sing, to tell our stories with a full-throated warble. As these poems navigate love and loss, they don't flinch from the highest or lowest notes. After all, as Vignali writes, "who would want to live / without fear, anyway? / Without a little bite of shame."

—Keetje Kuipers, author of *All Its Charms*, *The Keys to the Jail*, and *Beautiful in the Mouth*

Elizabeth Vignali's *House of the Silverfish* is bound together by repeating motifs: women—past and present, real and mythological, profiles of optometry patients, endangered animals, and an old house haunted by silverfish who remind it, the speaker, and the reader of our transience. In one of the first poems, "Mortgage," the speaker refers to "the earlier women whose room this was," and as I kept reading, I saw those earlier women everywhere—in the peeling wallpaper the silverfish devour, in "Medusa Washes the Windows," in the poems about mothers and daughters, in the central metaphor of the house. Vignali's honest, intimate voice holds all these threads together. But Vignali also knows when to let the images speak for themselves, like this one which concludes one of my favorite poems, "The Rule of Three":

"Outside, gathering dew, more laundry awaits. / Knee socks and shorts and swimsuits pinned / to the lilac, the medlar, the paperbark maple."

—Laura Read, author of *Dresses from the Old Country*, *Instructions for my Mother's Funeral*, and *The Chewbacca on Hollywood Boulevard Reminds Me of You*

HOUSE OF THE SILVERFISH

Elizabeth Vignali

HOUSE OF THE SILVERFISH
Copyright © 2021 Elizabeth Vignali
All Rights Reserved
Published by Unsolicited Press
Printed in the United States of America.
First Edition.

No part of this book may be used or reproduced in any manner whatsoever without written permission except in the case of brief quotations embodied in critical articles or reviews.

Attention schools and businesses: for discounted copies on large orders, please contact the publisher directly.

For information contact:
Unsolicited Press
Portland, Oregon
www.unsolicitedpress.com
orders@unsolicitedpress.com
619-354-8005

Cover Design: Kathryn Gerhardt
Cover Photo: Cover: Naomia Vignali
Editor: Caitlin James and S.R. Stewart

ISBN: 978-1-950730-73-5

HOUSE OF THE SILVERFISH

Contents

PART ONE
THERE WILL ALWAYS BE SOMETHING TO PAY FOR

MORTGAGE	3
Eve Picks the Apples	4
Mortgage	6
The Blue Whale	8
House of the Silverfish	10
Patient Profile: The Girl Who Accidentally Killed a Child With Her Car	12
Bloom: The Elephant Bed	14
Audubon's *Birds of America*, First Edition	16
Distributary	18
Golden Lion Tamarin	21
What If	23
The Phonograph	26
Homestead	28
Medea Does the Laundry	30
Mother's Day	31
THE POISONING	33
The Poisoning	34
One Step Forward, Two Steps Back	36

The Timber Wolf	38
Chantico Cooks Dinner	39
April Fool	40
Magpie	42
Her Reduction	44
The Valkyries Clear the Table	46
Kilauea, Redacted	49
As I Comb Lice from My Daughters' Hair	50
Light Loss	52

PART TWO
THERE WILL ALWAYS BE SOMETHING TO LOVE

WHAT'S LEFT	59
House of the Silverfish II	60
The Bug Man Says	62
The Rule of Three	64
Seated Nude, Viewed from the Back	66
What's Left	67
The Body Gifters	69
Medusa Washes the Windows	71
What I Would Have Said If I Were Shakespeare	72
The Ex-Lovers	73
The Sirens Take Out the Trash	75
Only One	77

The Fates Hang Wallpaper	78
Little House	79
Asase Yaa Pins Her Clothing On the Line	81
What the Eclipse Taught Me	82

SOMETHING SHINING UP   85

In the Side Yard	86
Jackie	87
House of My Mother	90
The Hippopotamus	92
Nocturne	94
Spring, As Directed by Alfred Hitchcock	97
Something Shining Up	98
As Soon As I Get Them	100
Reflection in the Window at the Redlight	102
Pluck	104
Girls in Doorways and Other Phenomena	105
Breaking Eggs	107
Shoal	110
Our Lady of the Silverfish	112

For my family.

"...but John says the very worst thing I can do is to think about my condition, and I confess it always makes me feel bad.

So I will let it alone and talk about the house."

—Charlotte Perkins Gillman, *The Yellow Wallpaper*

PART ONE

THERE WILL ALWAYS BE SOMETHING TO PAY FOR

MORTGAGE

"During the whole underside of her life, ever since her first memory, Eleanor had been waiting for something like Hill House."

—Shirley Jackson, *The Haunting of Hill House*

Eve Picks the Apples

Fecund Eden, half-bitten
      apples in our bellies.

We did not even get
      to finish our feast.

A coil of red, a hiss
      from an alphabet

that hadn't been written yet.
      A green explosion,

rainbow leaves.

      I tell my granddaughter

some people think
      her period pain is God's

punishment to me.

What about Grandpa,

she wants to know. And
    who would want to live

without fear, anyway?
    Without a little bite of shame.

Mortgage

Because I'm allowed to work for a living,
I know I must—if I'm to pay for this old house,
this old room with its cracked and peeling roses,
this post & pier lack of a foundation.
Mort from French for dead, *gage* for pledge,
linguists don't know if it's a promise to pay till death,
or the pledge is dead once paid, or the owner
is dead if unable to pay, and is no longer the owner.
The earlier women whose room this was
did not worry about paying for it; they weren't allowed
to. They washed cloth diapers with cracked and peeling
hands, leaned over the soup pot, steam congregating
as diamonds on their eyelashes. They serviced
their husbands who looked up at the pink ceiling
and worried about the mortgage until they went soft.

No, the women didn't have to worry about paying
for this house. They just loved their husbands
and if they didn't love their husbands, they loved
this house with its tapered ceilings and crooked floors

and if they didn't love the house, they loved
their children despite the grime and questions,
and if they didn't love their children, they loved
the garden, or at the very least the water running
beneath it, an old buried creek far below our feet
that carved the contours of the park down the road.
My grandmother said she saw it once, after Grandad
uprooted the old dead tree in the yard. She saw it down
there, running cold and swift beneath the house. Mortgage,
a promise from the dead: there will always be something
to pay for, there will always be something to love.

The Blue Whale

I was lamplight when night fell. I was speared
and flensed, minced and melted.

I was notched from upper jaw to tail fluke
with your insufficient rulers.

I was lather and varnish, fabric and rope.
I was corset, collar, whip, and toy.

You brought home my rorqual heart.
Displayed my boat-large parchment

skull in dusty museums.
You drove cars beneath my arched ribs.

But you could not catch my decibel moan,
my hymn to the silver path.

I am barnacle coven and seaweed plantation.
I am a salt-slapped planet to a thousand

open-mouthed moons. We sing louder than your engines. Despite the sonar shroud, we sing.

House of the Silverfish

      when we begin the ancient unraveling
          the ritual
of chew and swallow

when the wallpaper peels away
      in cigarette curls   when the book

falls apart in your hands
      when we lace the curtains
with moonlight   when

      we blink silver in the corners
          when we blister the paint
with our hunger

      when we eat paths
in your plaster
      when we slough the cracks wider

when you already know   nothing lasts

        but have managed to forget

            we will remind you
        with our quick-flash bodies

our bright burrowing spears

Patient Profile: The Girl Who Accidentally Killed a Child With Her Car

I teach her how to place the contact lens carefully
on the tip of her finger. To examine the flare
of its lip, make sure it curves in, not out. The lens
is lightly tinted blue for visibility. To make it easier
to see the small thing.

I know who she is. I imagine she knows I know,
is used to being the girl who looked at her phone
for a tragic instant. Read the internet comments
saying she deserves to die. Her pale lashes
are salt-slippery with saline, stuck together
in tiny blond mountain peaks. They escape her grasp
every time she brings the lens to her eye.

"It's the nature of the eye to close when something
is coming toward it," I say. "You have to override
your body's involuntary defense mechanism."
I show her how to pry her eye open by holding

the lid, not the lashes. Still, her eye squeezes shut
when it sees her finger approach.

"Sometimes it's easier not to look," I say, and show
her the trick of glancing away at the last minute,
the necessary distance her sensitive cornea needs.
It works. She adheres the contact to the white
of her eye. Air bubbles collapse with audible gasps.

The smallest of graces when she looks toward it,
the transparent shield slipping between her pupil
and the rest of the world.

Bloom: The Elephant Bed

after John Grade

They sleep to bloom, parchment trumpets of
pulp and filament, cream curves sinking into ink

and seawater. My daughters are only two and four,
but they sit as long as I do. They are under

the spell of the elephant bed. The white silence.
Massive prayers conjured solid but just barely,

translucent and whisper-light. The girls have
bruised knees and marker-smudged fingers,

pajama bottoms and brambled hair, but here
they aren't children. We three sit on the dark

marble floor and watch the pale sway of paper
and wire. It is before the black creeping.

Although there is some creeping in all of us,

even the littlest one. Even her cells, shoot-tender.

Audubon's *Birds of America*, First Edition

Fine shot and wires, the need to own
instead of observe. His gouache posing.

Audubon killed thousands of birds
in an effort to capture their images,

liked to paint them best when they weren't
quite dead yet. We were used to animals

lifeless—head on the wall, rug on the floor. Not
this living anointed by brush, the watercolor

and chalk Birds of America, vibrant alive
feathers and hearts still fighting for the beat,

undulled eyes watching the artist transpose
their image to paper. *How life-like!*

we marveled as we turned

the heavy cream pages as if it were

a catalog, picking out our favorite species
to wear as bright feathers in our hats.

Distributary

Woodlawn
Lakeview
Idlewild

we are drawn to the frocked photos
of ghost towns

of picnics with shawled
women in white dresses

their husbands'
mustaches

golden watch chains

to Echo Point by steamboat Rose
to White City by horseback

borders absorbed
less coal more mine

more lie than line

hotels dissolved to moss

Silver Beach
Blue Canyon City

there were names lost
before these were lost

but there are no parasol pictures of those

Golden Lion Tamarin

As if naivete was a virtue,
we waited till marriage,
voted Republican,
bagged our groceries in plastic.
Paid admission to
the small-town menagerie
of patchy-skinned parrots
and wan flamingoes. We
hooked casual fingers
in each other's belt loops
and strolled through
the heated butterfly garden,
lazuline wings
stuck to the floor like candy
wrappers. The golden
lion tamarins, the only real
life in the place. Their poppy-
bright fur. They're what we'd
remember years later, after
we heard the place had closed,

after we'd cheated on
each other and gone
liberal and bought reusable
shopping bags.
We didn't ask what
happened to them.
Were afraid to find out
we could have done something.
Instead we pictured them
back in the rainforest,
their small hands so much
like ours, peeling fruit
like a samba, offering
it to each other's mouths
as bitter oblations.

What If

In that other life, I teach piano;
you sell antiques: little moon-leafed
boxes and cobalt
blown-glass fishing floats
and musty brown medicine bottles
with remnants of sticky remedies.

You whistle home, wet with fern bouquets,
shoo rain beneath your boots.
I shake Chopin from my fingers
while you strum out the stars
and fry potatoes for dinner.
Moths loop silver infinities around the lamp.

You like my hair short
so you can kiss my neck.

We rise before the sun. Strawberries steep
in pockets, our hands
free for each other. We unfold

our red blanket
over brash spears of spring grass.

Clouds eat across the sky in caterpillar bites
while we discuss other lives we might have led.

Maybe you'd have a yellow cottage,
sweaters sprinkled with wood shavings,
a son with Victorian picture-book cheeks.

Maybe I'd have a daughter
who prefers her shoes on the wrong feet
and another who draws only horses.
Maybe a husband
who loves me in his own quiet way.

Maybe, happy as we'd be,
I'd sometimes drown
the what-ifs with too much wine.

Maybe you'd lie awake once
in a while
listening to rats

define a world in the walls.

The Phonograph

On Saturday afternoons
they brought the phonograph
outside the saloon
so the women and children
could listen, too,
to the brown wax cylinders
music-molded and sent spinning,
tinfoil tunes amplified
by walnut and brass.

Night was blacker then.
It could not be argued with.
The wax would not last,
or the thin plank sidewalk
lifting the saloon off the dirt,
or the man's hat resting
against the wall, or the woman
who leaned in the doorway,
her boot-tip inching from under
her long skirt, itching to tap.

After they posed for the photo,
they stepped into the street,
danced in the dirt road to the rushing
sound of the wax reel itself,
its steady hushed revolutions
magnified as much as the music,
a substantial *swish swish swish*
astonishingly like crinoline
or like the dead leaves
dashed under their feet.

Homestead

think of it
the small spaces they shared

a family of ten
in a one-room cabin

the sticky hands and open mouths

ten heads of hair
in need of brushing

the husband always wanting

Or the reverse—

the lone man homesteading
a patch of land the sky wide

he hasn't seen an unfurred face
in a thousand days

uses his voice only
so it doesn't wander away

thinks sometimes
of letting the winter
bury his loneliness with snow

while the mother of eight
turns her face to the wall

and pretends she doesn't hear the asking

Medea Does the Laundry

So this is what it's come to. A pink sock frowning
over my hand, dirt-sneered tighty-whities in the hamper.
My palms, once lined with sorcery and opium,
now gather detergent in chemical creases. Remembered
parts circle and whir in the water, dismembered feet
and torsos and pairs of legs swimming through a storm
of synthetic clean that doesn't smell like any
mountain breeze I've ever known. I forgot
to check the pockets again. The children's gathered
treasures escape: pennies and pinecones and orphaned
beach rocks. They clamor at the door. They rattle
like an army of teeth.

Mother's Day

It's Mother's Day. The robin that woke me up
is going gangbusters. Chirp chirp chirrup chirp.
Robins always sound a little drunk to me,
like they're just figuring it out as they go along.
Wavery and unmelodic and not giving a shit
about the song sparrows and Swainson's
thrush and their flawless intricate flourishes.

Years ago, scientists who were studying nature
versus nurture isolated birds pre-hatch to see
what kind of call they might have. What kind
of song. The birds hatched and never knew
a mother. Never saw another bird. They lived
their whole lives in solitude with only the unkindness
of people for company, and still they sang
imperfect songs, for sure, sometimes a missed
note or extra trill—but they all sang the distinctive
song of their species without ever being taught.

My mother's favorite bird was the chickadee.
She chose chickadees for her headstone, two
figures engraved in rock, a pair of granite birds
atop a granite pine branch. When it rains, the water
fills the lines of their bodies, their tiny wings,
miniscule rivers with black beds, rainwater sheen
making the birds look like they're moving, a little.
Alive as long as the rain keeps falling.

I don't know what kind of bird the scientists used
for their study. Probably something with a more
reliable song than the robin's. Probably something
with a more complicated tune than the chickadee's
two-note melody. It called and called, followed all the rules
of nature that said if you sing, somewhere, somehow,
someone will answer.

THE POISONING

where everything

in this house has long been over,
kettle and mirror, spoon and bowl,
including my own body...
  —Margaret Atwood, "Morning in the Burned House"

The Poisoning

I heard once of a man and woman off the coast of
    California
found dead in their small boat with a faulty propane stove.
Adrift for days, they still sat across from each other,
her fingers curled
around the stem of an empty wineglass, his cheek
pressed against the playing cards
on the table
between them.

She would have gone first, with her small lungs.

I wonder if he knew it was over.
If he noticed her gaze slip away,
her coldness,
right before he recognized
his own torpor.

The people who found them discovered a baby
squalling in the stern

far enough from her parents
to be safe.

It happens that way, sometimes:
the failure, the slow seep.
The only ones left alive
the children.

One Step Forward, Two Steps Back

I wear your feet around my neck,
a pair of fleshy weights
with rope tied round the ankles.

They sometimes kick
against me, sometimes sway,
a sickle moon.
They thump my chest
as I roll out pie dough
& tiptoe in circles over the grass
while I twist dandelion roots from the lawn.

When I sit, your feet brush my lap
like children waiting for a story.
When I raise my arms
in the shower,
your toes crevice under my breasts
like mice.

I'd give them back to you
but they've gone soft
& black around the ankles,
your toes purple & wrinkled
like grapes
forgotten in the fridge
behind the mayonnaise
& milk.

The Timber Wolf

In this version, she's still not easy to love. In this version,
she stalks your pets, not your children. Her indifference
cuts you. Her unflinching yellow eyes. She's no

shoeshine deer, no lapsed sheep. In this version, she ignores
Little Red Riding Hood, her talcumed grandmother.

She brings bones to the den, licks her cubs' noses wet,
cradles her lover in the furred scoop of her body.
She's no character in your story, villain or otherwise.

Which makes you—in this version—not the hero.

So shear your sheep. Call your scraping dogs. Surround
yourself with barbed wire and the beasts who adore you,

as if those who are easy to love were worth the loving.

Chantico Cooks Dinner

how tough does it have to be
how skillet-shy

how long has it been
scaled and curling under my knife
how does it unfurl
      its green and white

how rough it tongues
      an ardent sheen
how it embosses its wings with rain

a slub in wool
              a lump in cloth

and snails painting the maize silver

how many years
      the skillet spiced
           with reasons

April Fool

Today I wonder if I could take it back
as if all minor and major losses were a bad joke.
My daughter's missing jacket would shine blue
from the long line of empty school hooks
and my favorite mug would reappear,
its perfect swooped handle nestled
among the rows of lesser handles.
The airplane uncrashes
and within its painted casing
the man with thinning hair sighs and crosses his legs
ice rattles in plastic cups
the black-eyed woman worries
her husband will forget to pick up the kids.
Mud slides back up the hill
and unburies the old couple
watching TV in their matching corduroy armchairs
and the man wiping fingerprints from his glasses
and the woman in her burgundy sedan
who turns the radio knob from news to music
because she doesn't want to think

about all those poor people on the plane.
Pens would be found, milk unspilled,
scabs erased from pink knees.
You would lie beside me
wreathed in your regular breath
not knowing I didn't love you.

Magpie

In the pasture, the magpies flip cow-shit patties over
with their feet and collect beetles: darkling, burying,
>   milkweed, dung.
They feed their babies in the twig-tangle nest they built
together. He shaped the sticks, she smoothed mud into the
>   cup,
lined it with grass. The stream is dark with minnows
and sludge. Semi-trucks herd the highway in the distance,
bric-a-brac boxes hauling Doritos and patio chairs.
Last week when the birds lost one of their own to the road,
>   they
flocked around the fallen one, brought offerings
of grass and insects. Her offspring's black bills nudged her
>   body,
mouths infant-pink when they opened them to cry for her.
Animal behaviorists say if we call this grief, we're
>   anthropomorphizing.
Occam's razor says the correct answer is the most obvious
>   one.

When it comes to conservation, magpies are classified as
of least concern. Once again here I am,
writing another endangered animal poem
about an animal that isn't endangered.
Maybe I just want the vulnerable to take note.
See the way magpies switched from picking ticks
off bison to swiping flies from cattle after the mass kill-off,
how they've learned to recognize the faces of people
who have harmed them. Study up on adapting
when pasture turns into Home Depot and ranchers
shoot them on sight. Move from trees to telephone poles.
Build nests in warehouses.
When all else fails, know how to mourn.

Her Reduction

It's the solo ferry ride, of all things,
that makes me realize I'm alone.
The unsunblocked patch
on my back, not having to listen
to Tom Petty, finishing a chapter.

The lovers fetch each other's sweatshirts
from the car and smile
at their cameras. They align
shoulders to measure the constancy

of the horizon. They ask each other how
much longer till we get there.
Josephine Baker breezes along
through my earbuds.

Her voice cracks on I.
I wonder whether she and I can be we
or if the glaucous-winged gulls
with their careening blackless feathers

can be we or if the grains of sand
lisping beneath my shoes can be we.

The moon scrubbed down to scarfskin
and the lovers claiming even her reduction.

Even the scant of her white eyelash.

The Valkyries Clear the Table

The heroes have autographed the table again
with their glasses, rings of condensation
in looped cursive circles that interrupt

each other's epics. We take turns
riding to the shoreline
to measure the water's rise.

Bide our time until the earth
gets swallowed up. The heroes have retired
to the other room. They watch football—

muddy boots on the coffee table,
shields and spears stacked by the door
just in case the wolf starts howling

and the stars go out. We clear away
the latest carnage. No souls for us anymore,
just chicken bones and Cheeto crumbs,

plates globbed with seven-layer dip
and hot-wing sauce red as blood.
The heroes cry out—

a foul in the game, another penalty.
They call for more mead, more beer.
Use their daggers to sweep the dirt

from under their nails.
Tell each other they would have
done it this way or that way

if they were the players. Gods
miscast as humans. The cheerleaders
smile and shake their pompoms.

We lift the heroes' crusted heels,
wipe the filth from their soles.
Ask if they need anything else.

We bring the heroes' half-empty pitchers
to the sea: flat Pabst and Coors Light
and too-sweet honey mead.

We empty it all into the waves,
gauge the horizon's glassy intentions,
and measure the water again.

Kilauea, Redacted

      beneath our feet
our shadows are as big as gods

      the cloud
leans her forehead against the mountain

she thinks she will always be alone

      by the lagoon
the trees bloom with white birds

there are snakes here

      but you would not know them
if you saw them

As I Comb Lice from My Daughters' Hair

I squeak the fine-toothed comb through wet tresses
drenched in olive oil. I use my grandpa's old ivory
toothpick to free the wedged bodies, a vintage little sword
that once speared martini olives and now slays lice.
I drown them in hot water, float them in a blue cereal bowl.

We call in sick to school and work
and watch Judy Garland movies all day: *Harvey Girls*,
Meet Me in St. Louis, *The Wizard of Oz*. My daughters
take turns teetering on the tall stool with a *National
    Geographic*
pushed under the short leg. They squeal whenever I find a
    louse.

We shampoo again and again. We drink hot chocolate and
    sing
"Over the Rainbow." They can't tell the difference between
the mustachioed actors in *Harvey Girls* and keep asking
which is the good one and which is the bad. "That's the one

we think is bad who turns out to be good," I say.

Or "That's the one we think is good who turns out to be
    bad."
The dark lice sink to the bottom of the bowl. The nits float
    on top,
translucent eggs nested in a golden oil slick.
They are almost as white as the snow outside.
They are almost as white as the villain's teeth.

Light Loss

my daughter arranges the glass panes
in a cardboard box
with a hole chopped in it

little windows
lucid domino-shapes
she shines
her light through

and it seems
that light should make
some sort of sound
when passing through glass

an audible tinkle
of magic happening

but this is not magic

just a science project
measuring the passage
of light
through varying
thicknesses
of glass

particles or waves
particles and/
or waves

how much light is lost
through a square

a rectangle

how much
is lost through one pane
two panes
three panes
four

is more light lost
through windows

of rooms
we don't want
to see into

does light
have consciousness

does it shy away
from one
and stream toward another

when the shades are drawn
for the drill
at my daughter's school

and she hides
in the reading corner
behind bright
beanbag chairs

knees tucked to her chest
so as to make the smallest
smaller

does she take comfort
in the rules of science
and light, the beloved
consistency of flashlight
and pencil

the light plays along
with my daughter's
experiment

does the expected thing
when she measures
lumens with the light-
meter

she records diminishing
numbers
in the notebook
under her hypothesis
"more panes lead to lost light"

I picture the light lost
among the surfaces of glass

wandering around
in particles and/or waves

holding each other's
hands and saying

we will find it
we will find the way out

PART TWO

THERE WILL ALWAYS BE SOMETHING TO LOVE

WHAT'S LEFT

A door, a chair,
the sea.
The limitless, inconstant
whiteness
of the wall. The few lines
that hold it together.

—Coral Bracho, "From this Light,"
Translated by Forrest Gander

House of the Silverfish II

we loved too, once— a river of silver
        faces nearly touching

                stepped forward, stepped back
too close, too far away

        spindled brittle, a needle
to prick your finger on, sew
            your eyes open

a slither of shining bodies
        in the windowsill, memory of damp
            memory of

        our cave beneath the flaking paint
his gossamer bargain

the taste of wallpaper paste, of plaster,
                    glue, thread, the silk
        ribbons your grandmother left

                    like yours, our family lives
on what holds this house
            together

The Bug Man Says

The bug man says
there are no wasps in my house.
I follow him while he checks corners,
unscrews light fixtures, runs his fingers
along flaking windowsills. I usually overlook
this clutter: the juice glass in the closet—dust huddled
at the bottom like refugee pulp—bobby pins, books,
my daughter's obsessive origami cranes
on every flat surface. The black garbage bags
on top of the armoire, untouched for six years,
bulging with my late mother's belongings.

He unfolds his ladder in what was once her room.
The top half of his body disappears
into the attic where I've never been.
He is in a magician's box, his body divided
by what I know and what I don't.
From below, I can see his flashlight's beam.
Shadows cross its careless slicing,
suture the wounds with immediate darkness.

When he descends, the trapdoor sighs closed
as if the space had never been illuminated.

In the garage, we find a lone yellow jacket.
She pulls herself along the workbench layered
with sawdust and grime. Her legs are heavy
and listless in the dim air. "She's a queen,"
the bug man says. "See how fat with eggs she is?"
He's found a yellowed newspaper in the corner.
*Egypt and Israel Sign Formal Treaty, End Thirty Years
of War*, it says. He brushes the wasp to the floor.
He intends to crush her with his thick-soled boot,
but she vanishes in wood shavings and leaf debris.
Alive, somewhere. A striped and tired crescent moon.

The Rule of Three

My two daughters fold laundry
and listen to an album of fairy tales while I crack
yesterday's Easter eggs for sandwiches.

It's late. The children
of married mothers are in bed,
fed and bathed and read to.

I drink red wine and roll an egg
between my palms until the crayon pink bunny
fractures like an ancient fresco.

Why is it always three?
my oldest daughter asks. She
has folded a towel neatly in half, in half,

in half again. *The three little pigs,
The three bears, the three billy goats gruff.
Why is it never two or four?*

I say, *There's something about threes.*
The brain finds it satisfying. She squints
her eyes. She is nine. Nothing is satisfying.

They've done studies, I say. I wait
to see if this is enough. The eggs in neat
concentric slices, yellow and white

1950s wallpaper on toast. Salt shivers
from the shaker. Tap water plink plink
plinks from the faucet I don't know how to fix.

Her little sister straightens the stack, says,
The question is, why is it always
the biggest or the richest or the prettiest?

Outside, gathering dew, more laundry awaits.
Knee socks and shorts and swimsuits pinned
to the lilac, the medlar, the paperbark maple.

Seated Nude, Viewed from the Back

Is a woman still a woman, even in pen and ink? Consider the curves. A scratching thin as a violin's wail implies voluptuousness, invites your imagined hand to rest just there, on the trailing slope of her hip. Yet, she is only a handful of lines spare as winter. No bright oils soothe her scraped furrows, no pastels. Not even the pedestrian touch of a watercolor brush. A child could count her lines on his fingers and toes. She is an implication, so scarce your hand might pass right through her. Does she know she will only ever be a sketch? Matisse will add nothing: no vase of wilted tulips, no poppy-printed blanket, no open window. Not even a touch of pink for her back. She is just a study, a shape hinted with a few careless strokes.

Yes, she knows. Knows she is nothing but this scattering of scratches, knows she's composed of borders that could have bound anything, knows she must hold herself together, clutch her borrowed lines. Legs crossed, arms tucked, head down—if she opens her hand, lifts it from her thigh, she will fly apart. She will be a tree, a moon, a flock of birds.

What's Left

Eurasian reed warbler to the cuckoo chick

The hollows of what would have been
my children pock the mud in mucky swallows—
not even the clamor of shattered shell
or broken bones, just the gulping absences
sunk among reeds and sweet-grass.

You are what's left to me.
You overflow the nest with your bawdy
striped breast and brash-budding hawk beauty.
I bring you leopard moths and rove beetles. I sing
you my drab brown song.

You gape your mouth
bigger than my head
and demand more.

I didn't know it would be so hard
to love you. I strive for connection while you sleep,

try to imagine you grown, wonder if I have
the same miscreant black feathers
hidden beneath my chest.

What kind of mother am I, doling out meals
with resentment lodged in my throat?
What miserly hand carved out my stature,
my flea-sized heart?

When I search for anything resembling
affection, all I see is my own tiny eye
engulfed like a stone
in the wide pool of yours.

The Body Gifters

Aunt Jenny tells us Aunt Jenny is gone.
Now, she's Antoinette: a star child, a stranger,
an alien who traveled from some far-off planet
and phased into Aunt Jenny's offered body.

I don't know the details—whether she steamed to Earth
on a meteor or teleported in a column of blue Star Trek
        particles
or came on a spaceship with a hundred sister aliens
who now occupy other aunts' bodies.

Regardless, it is now Antoinette who stretches to fill
Aunt Jenny's skin. She browsed organs, scanned molecular
structures, prodded the thick fingers of optic nerves,
and flipped through corded tendons
with the expertise of a seasoned buyer.

Antoinette traded sunspots for liver spots, distant galaxies
for a Ford Galaxie. She colors Aunt Jenny's platinum
hair, paints her nails fuchsia, props star-studded

rhinestone sunglasses over her glaucomatous eyes.
She rifles through shifting memories
and throws out the broken ones.

Dad calls her "eccentric" when he's being kind,
"crazy" when he's not. He prefers a loss
he can understand. I like my losses less concrete.

When I call her on her birthday, Antoinette says she has
Aunt Jenny's memories of me. She remembers that hot
Portland summer when I was thirteen, my too-short shorts,
the onion bagels I smeared with marmalade, The Cure
playing through my perpetual headphones.

After we hang up, I catch myself testing my own interior
swivel corneas across the pink-mapped membranes
of my inner eyelids, hitch the breath hot in my lungs.

I press my fingers to the dull ache that swells
my throat when depression floods my body.
How nice to give it all up.
To welcome in someone who really wants it.

Medusa Washes the Windows

Snakes don't like ammonia; it scorches their scent-
seeking tongues, burns their many pebbled eyes.

Instead I use vinegar, that piss-acrid homely solution,
the hiss of spit and clean. Acid and newspaper,
like my mother taught me. Like her mother passed on
to her.

Their palms, too, blackened with bad news.
The clench and rumple of headlined sheets,
a man's world striped with conquest.

My hands couldn't hold him back, but they can do this:
spray and wipe and wait for someone
to look past their own cursed reflection
to find me inside.

What I Would Have Said If I Were Shakespeare

A brambly catch, with your lackluster back
brackish in a forgettable corner. Laggard
milkfish. Creep up on me now. Won't you
try it, ashen Prometheus? Stingy figure—
show me your grey eyes, your sack full of sticks.
Meet me in my corner. Stinted mammal.
Overstayed ghostweed. Here is your necrotomy,
your linear track, your peccable terrain.
Here is the door. Here is
your fulminant reputation.

THE EX-LOVERS

"When someone shows you who they are, believe them the first time."

—Maya Angelou

"Well, if there's that many, they'll probably get us wherever we are."

—Ben in *Night of the Living Dead*

They have risen again, not in any insightful way
but because that's what they do.

Instinct kicked in right after the credits,
a lumbering, awkward hunger they don't know
how to fill. They thirst for a sequel.

They move their dead feet through the wet grass.
They could be a painting, here in the rain,
uniform in their blues and greys. A watercolor de-
composition.

They need money, they need
a favor, they need that book they lent you.
They squint in your windows and leave
cheeks glued to the glass. They need to know why
you didn't change your number.

They need to know if that is an invitation.

They leave fingernails in your front door.
They ask if you're remembering
to water the plants.

They say they were just in the neighborhood.

"Braaaaaains," they say.
They need your mind. They need to know
they could change it
if they wanted to.

The Sirens Take Out the Trash

The morning smells like freshly baked bread
and low-tide sea creatures. Someone whistles
for their dog. Someone asks for their coffee to go.
Someone strums out a Sam Cooke song on the guitar.

We listen to tourists' footsteps on the boardwalk above
and cup our terrible song in fingers stained with seaweed
and nicotine. We cringe from sunlight striped
across our skin and bury our eyes in sand until dusk.

Float planes buzz and jostle over the water like wasps.
Shredded cabbage confettis through the boardwalk cracks
from fish tacos and veggie burgers.
The wind tastes like oil and oysters.

When night falls and lampposts blossom orange
along the pier, we creep up to the rocks that used to be ours
and release our voices to the wind.
They're too weak now to reach far.

Our song tangles in fishnets and eel grass. It ricochets
in crab pots and eddies around tide pools rainbow-slick
with gasoline. We patch our voices with tar and duct tape.
We tie them together with stray shoelaces.

We call our longing to the fleet of commuter ferries.
Cathlamet, Elwha, Hiyu, Sealth.
Family, plenty, animal, stone.
Someone balls up a red-and-white food wrapper

and casts it in the harbor.
Our voices summon the rubbish: coke bottles and buttons
and plastic bags, waxed paper and nylon fishing line. The
     red
pockmarked faces of buoys.

We used to have standards.
The strong chests of kings and fishermen.
Once, poets brought us words and verses in golden chains.
Once, sailors offered us their throats.

Only One

He's the original Adam, cable-knit sweater pulled down
over his missing rib. He's thinking about ending things

with Eve—not because he doesn't love her, I mean God,
look at their history—but because he can't remember

what it was like before he had this slack fleshy gap
in his bones, a tender fontanelle that seems to invite

every sharp counter corner and heedless bicycle handlebar
and other glancing jabs, like the absence of notches

on his bedpost and numbers in the little black book
with page after page of inkless lines. It prompts him

to prod the hollow lamella over his cartilaginous cage,
to wonder if this perpetual stitch will ever ossify

and heal the horrible discomfort of knowing
there is only one woman who was made for him.

The Fates Hang Wallpaper

We furl and uncurl, dip, and brush. We cut. We align
paper roses seam to seam, pink petals lipped edge
to edge, shadow to shadow, light to light. Leaf
leaps to leaf across invisible crevices. We unspool
paper in whispering strips. We slacken, we straighten.
We cut. If we do our job right (and we always do),
you'll never know it could have been otherwise.
Leaf might have given way to rose, petal to thorn,
stem to sky. Atropos unrolls the length of paper.
Clotho lacquers the wall with acrid glue. Lachesis
shears it off. Even we have our small rebellions.

Little House

You are Mary and I am Laura
and Jack is our pet tornado
churning across the berm.

He twists up grass
and a murmuration of starlings.
He twists up a swarm of locusts.

We loop dirty fingers
and walk to the tracks
wait for the train
our toes nudged against the steel
like a dare.

Weather balloons float
to the surface of the sky
rising like Ma's golden vanity cakes
and I remember suddenly the way
Ma used to iron

her hands smooth
while she waited for Pa
to walk through the door
full of sunlight and wheat dust.

But that was a long time ago
and now
inside the tornado
the birds are still singing.

Asase Yaa Pins Her Clothing On the Line

For you think, it's only a clothesline. But let's
let its anonymity go; let's admit there's the line you see
and the line you don't. Let's build
a profile: I'm a size 16, my fibers natural,
my waistbands elastic, my underwear practical.
My colors run cool like beach glass, blues
and greens that whirl and eddy in the wind. But
a long red dress breaks your projected pattern, trips
you up like a loose step on the stairway—
my long red dress with my invisible head nodding
to mythical music. Yoga pants dance and inexplicable
scarves full of the stars flap smoke signals from me to you,
a message from April, a lingering spring translation.
Holey cashmeres and too-buttoned cardigans climb
the line like a stairway back to December. A calendar
less constant than the stars, but yet—that dress—
that long red dress with a blue refrain.

What the Eclipse Taught Me

If you get five out of six numbers correct in the lottery, you're still a loser.

—Fred Espenak, "Mr. Eclipse"

88% is a lot, nearly the whole
thing. The black moon sliding
over the sun like a manhole
cover, a heavy mineral disc left
ajar. But shadow-chasers say
totality makes all the difference.
I wouldn't know, never having
experienced anything but
the almost, the mostly,
the not quite. Still, 88%
isn't bad, I'll take it, I guess—
examine the shadows closer
than usual, the sickle
suns scattered across
the leafy asphalt. I'll glance

up at that bare sliver of light—
just 12%, the merest scrap—
a white curve of flame just
bright enough to prevent
me from seeing the stars.

SOMETHING SHINING UP

"We started selling and counting. Anything from earthworms and bottles to paper shell pecans. She saved green stamps and we ate pinto beans from dented cans. She found a house with bramble bushes. We found a lovely alley made dizzy circles. We found a house with attic rooms."

—Harryette Mullen, "She Swam On from Sea to Shine"

In the Side Yard

creeping jenny
false solomon

rust and lichen sprawled across
the demolished shed

avalanche and fawn lily
shooting stars

a blue mop bucket filled with rainwater
and newly hatched dragonflies

foxgloves
forgotten gloves

and the tree frog in the broken pot
beating like a green heart

JACKIE

3am and awake because of the woman who called
and asked for Jackie. *You have the wrong number*, I'd said,
and hung up. I can't go back to sleep because of the
    expectation
in her voice, like she was all jacked up on crying
and had planned out what she was going to say.
I want you back or *I'm finally leaving Joe*
or *How could you steal Joe from me?*

I listen to the train's wheels ringing down the tracks
by the water. I wonder if she got ahold of Jackie
or if she'd used up her determination with the wrong call.
Now she flicks the long column of ash from her cigarette
or now she lies next to Joe, her suitcase back in the closet,
or now she lies next to where Joe used to be before he got
    drunk
and kissed Jackie at the company Christmas party.

When I was a kid, our phone number was one digit
    different

from the taxi company's. Every night after the bars closed,
drunks woke us with their slurred requests, consonants
    running together
like smudged chalk. This was back when there were still
    phone booths
and the scratched plastic-sheathed book hanging on its
    heavy silver rope.
Dialing an 8 instead of a 3 was small on the scale of
    mistakes
they could make depending on how their evening was
    going.

Once when my mom answered the phone
the woman started crying. *This is my last quarter*, she'd said.
Mom put on her shiny white polyester robe and drove
    downtown
where the woman waited outside the phone booth by the
    3B tavern.
This was back when there were still phone booths
and the 3B and Mom. She drove the woman home.
She told her to always carry two quarters.

It's been an hour since the woman called for Jackie.
Now she slides her sore feet back into her white nurse's

      shoes
or now she watches the fill and spill of Joe's sleeping breath
or now she finally falls asleep herself, her hand buried
      between her thighs.
My mom wouldn't have hung up. *Tell me about Jackie*,
she would have said. I lie awake and listen to the silence
after the train, thinking about how I used to think
its whistle at night was the loneliest sound in the world.

House of My Mother

Back when spotted towhees were rufous-sided
and Pluto was a planet, my mother played marbles

in the yard with her brothers. She filled sturdy glasses
with water straight from the tap; cleaned polish

from her nails, the acetone slide of erasure; curled
her peroxide blond into a flip. She watched her mother

slice tomatoes on the Formica countertop and picked
at the patches of lead paint peeling off the windowsill

until they were continents, until they were worlds,
white beneath her fingernails. Back before chemo,

before breastless. Back when breathless was a metaphor.
Now I say goodnight to my daughters in what was once

her room. Paint latex over lead, change the charcoal
filter on the faucet, chop organic tomatoes on

a bamboo cutting board. We only know what we know.
My mother used to help her father shower the lawn

with fertilizer green from a plastic bag. When we lever
up the sod to put in a patio, the marbles are still there,

dozens of them. Planets swirled blue-green in the dirt,
a galaxy put to rest beneath the perfect grass.

The Hippopotamus

Rainy season, rising water, flood fingering the woods,
the cusp of valley. Miombo, mopane, spangled bowers
of jesse-bush. In the dream I ride downstream
on a hippopotamus, a river-horse from the ancient Greek.
Water overwhelms the hard brink of land.

Hippos are vulnerable rather than endangered, or so we've
decided. So we can wait, as is our way, until the last
minute. *Vulnerable* from the Latin noun *vulnus*, wound.
Once, it was a Janus word; cupped two meanings:
capable of being wounded and capable of wounding.

Oxbow, island, sandbank, pool. This aquatic mammal's
closest relations are whales and dolphins. They live
in water: sex in the river, birth in the lake. But the rain
brings so little these days. A few diminishing puddles,
and so many to fight for it. We all are capable of wounding.

So yes, they're vulnerable. These herbivores kill more people
each year than all the African predators combined. As blue

gives way to gold; green to brown. They yearn toward
        gentle, but
the world won't allow it. I get it. I know what it is to eschew
flesh in favor of green and still cause harm everywhere I go.

In the dream, there is plenty of water. I am vulnerable
and I long for her skin, the thickest of all the mammals.
Her lunges plume the river, spells in bubbles to her lover:
I want you. Bracken fern, morning mist, evening dew.
When I dream, I lower my mouth to the river.

Nocturne

I
I warm my hands with a tin cup
hot with chocolate and rum,
keep vigil under the lunar eclipse
while the children conjure the maundering
bats; they throw stones in the water
and up in the air to summon
the wild inky creatures.

They circle the subdued moon with small fingers,
sure of their dominion.

See the slick and shiny part? one says
to the other. *That's the moon smiling.*

II
Somewhere in the ocean right now
there's a warm-blooded moonfish,
tinfoil skin so thin a fingernail
can scrape it away,

fins red as though
he has already been speared.

Even science can't explain
how he heats not only
the cold blood in his veins
but also the ocean around him—
how he wills his heart hot.

III
The match pins light to the tip
of my cigarette, an illicit ash lamp
outside my sleeping daughters' window
under the blue bowl of sky
chipped with stars.

The eclipse is ending
and the sun's light salvages
the moon from earth's shadow,
parcels out the gleam
in luminous increments.
I tell myself I'm not lingering
to see if I, too, am worth saving.

IV
Moonfish,
you bring the night with you like a gift,
cup it in your cool hands, carry it
in the pockets of the jacket you
press against my sleepy indoor skin.

You are still sleeping
when I get up in the dark
of early morning.
You sleep like one
who wants to be caught.

The moon is so bright
my retina makes room for it.

A semi-permanent shape:
everywhere I look

there's a moon.

Spring, As Directed by Alfred Hitchcock

Someone is whistling in the dark alleys
left over from winter. The soggy ditch where green
hasn't reached yet, or the thicket growing over
the gutter. A chickadee, maybe, eyes
buried in the shadow of his black fedora,
his seesaw whistle lonely like a rusty swing
penduluming on an empty playground. The sun
shines, forsythia crawls open along
its yellow branch, robins press their flushed breasts
to the dirt and listen for breakfast.
They would have us believe everything
is okay. But the worms are furtive.
The red-winged blackbird's shoulders flash
like red herrings. The crows cough into their black
sleeves and plan their next move.

Something Shining Up

If it weren't for the air frothed thick with lilacs,
it would feel like August. The lawn under my bare feet
still warm from the sun, even beneath the moon's round
      face.
It's nearly one a.m., late for this morning girl,
but I couldn't sleep with the laundry out and rain coming.

The clothespins mooring the sheets to the line
are warm to the touch, the heavy white towels rough-dried
and stiff as sails as they lift in the growing breeze.
The moon stirs in the wind like something
shining up from the bottom of the ocean.

It's nearly nine a.m. in Ireland right now. An eight hour
difference between us, added to all the usual differences.
We are at opposite ends of what we tend towards:
you the ponderer of late nights, I the dawn riser.
The packer of lunches, hair braider, toast butterer.

But for now, the lunch eaters are sleeping. You
are waking up, or brewing coffee, or making love
to someone else. What a strange April this is.
The moon warm on my back. The scent of lilacs
so strong I feel them like hands on my shoulders.

As Soon As I Get Them

As soon as I get them
I give them away

This one is a fork in the road
      This one breathes underwater
            This one rubs my blood between his fingers

Forest of hands

This one is salt scraped from the seafloor
      This one is yolk on my chin
            This one broke my only ladder

In the corner
the new couple

arms around waists
heads on shoulders

Take his double tongue
Take his cracked blessings
Take his belly off my back
Take his eyes on the mirror
Take his jackpot jaw
Take his bruised box apples

I read somewhere that because electrons
have a negative charge
we can never actually touch anything

Reflection in the Window at the Redlight

Her transparent hands lift
pockets of blankness

and set them alight, bright
flames birthed in reflection.

This methodical heft and lift
and flick of the red Bic lighter

is her bar-back ritual, sacred
rite at the Redlight.

The best part of her day:
when she raises

her tray of a dozen fires,
bright flickering hymns.

When she gifts stars
to every dark table.

PLUCK

Only she knows why she chose the mailbox
over easier incubators,
why she endured the white slices of envelopes
mass ads flopped in inky curls
the latest celebrity's glossy stare.

When we bullied out her careful twigs
and dumped them daily under the azaleas,
she chose new branches and arranged them
as patiently as if each time were the first.

She ignored the postman's knuckles on her breast,
the tidal flux of mail mayhem.
She fluffed her nest with wiry puffs of yellow insulation,
silvered scraps of plastic bags

and the best feathers
torn from her own chest,
her fierce obstinate love insisting:
This. This. This. This.

Girls in Doorways and Other Phenomena

I stop in the middle of cleaning
out the refrigerator to play with my children.
Expired yogurt sweats on the counter.
A vinegar-soaked rag weeps a puddle

into the wilted kale arching against its yellow
paper twist-tie. My daughters and I, each
in our own doorways, press the backs
of our hands hard against our respective

doorjambs, arm muscles straining,
and begin to count. They have only just learned
this first trick of the body: the way their arms,
after being released from pressure, will fly up

of their own accord. Kohnstamm phenomenon.
The littlest is in the china closet
with the translucent plates and hyacinth teacups
because her arms are too short

for a regular doorway. Her big sister
is in the passage to the back porch.
From here, I can see chickadees in the purple
lilac. My oldest daughter's closed-lipped smile,

denim stretched across the tenuous notion
of hips. The paper-blanketed table:
school newsletters and crayon drawings and
magazines and bills. Bread-crumb constellations

across the linoleum. One pink
sneaker, its upturned sole matted
with wet grass. Even after the kettle
unfurls its high song on the stove,

we count to sixty. Then we let go
and step forward. Watch each other's faces
while our arms rise as if magicked weightless.
Rise and rise like unstoppable wings.

Breaking Eggs

I've invited my ex-husband over for dinner
but when he arrives, I haven't even started yet.
Instead, I'm collaging with my daughters, elbow-deep
in glue sticks and scattered scraps of magazines.
He is too good to show that he expects nothing less,

that he has never asked me to be anyone
but who I am. He walks to the kitchen, rummages
through cupboards for the cheese grater. He's already
forgotten where it is. I roll out pie dough
while he slices asparagus in precise green segments.

Last night he texted me that the lady he was seeing
is seeing someone else. Now we say nothing about it.
I press dough into the pan's ruffled edges and pour
him a glass of wine. He cores a bell pepper
and pinches white seeds from its crisp yellow.

A knock at the door once we get the quiche in the oven,
neighbors returning a dish from their Saturday party.

They are not surprised to see us together. We are the
    models,
the no-longer-couple who are doing this admirably.
They didn't notice when we left their party for a walk

around the neighborhood, a rare chance to talk without
the kids. He told me about his lady, that he was worried
something was wrong. I told him about the phone call,
after over a year, from the man who'd had a hand
in ending our marriage. Or—let's be honest—

not exactly a hand, but a less monogamously acceptable
    part.
How he'd called, needing a favor. "You should do it,"
my ex said. "Be the bigger person." And this is why
I fell in love with him, why I love him even now, though
not in the way we both wish I did. He knows how to be

the bigger person while I struggle with knowing
how to be a person at all. But now the neighbors leave
and the quiche has leaked out of the bottom of the cracked
pan, an eggy mess on the oven floor. Our children come in
with grass-green knees and lilac blossoms in their hair.

They are hungry. I break the eggs, he slices bread
and fries up sausage patties. What's left of the ruined
quiche steams on the counter. The late sun tints all of us
orange through the open front door while we eat,
standing up, scrambled eggs for dinner.

Shoal

It starts with the hemistich hitch in her step.
A henchwoman's tell, regret stopping up the gait

with sediment. This moon's stepdaughter can't keep
swindling tarot cards and sneaking roofies

into her own whiskey-gingers, back tattooed
with bedsheet creases from sleeping till noon.

But she hates hesitation the most. Bring it back or don't:
the bar's blurry disciples, whispered skirmish

of kisses, the fingertips brushing the strings
secret as any affair. This mystery has outstripped

a thousand others: that she will still prostrate
herself for muchness. She will shove aside

her heretic intuition and angle into the swivel-hipped
wind, shrug her shoulder through the neck

of her sloppy blue dress, a shoal emerged
from the ocean, heart bare no matter the tide.

Our Lady of the Silverfish

You find the cracks for me—the small space
behind the triangle of peeling wallpaper,

the crevice in the plaster, the air between
one page and the next. O Lady, show me

the hidden. Silver splash stacked among
the good china. The shine between piano

keys, bathroom towels, floorboards, grout.
Powder through the holes in my curtains.

Paint the dark corners bright, soften all
hard surfaces. Nothing is impervious

to your diminishing, your glinting familiars.
O Lady, you gleam unseen, shine for no one

but yourself. When I bought this house,
pulled up the carpet to find the padding

below gone to chemical yellow dust, you
bestowed your first teaching. O Lady, I am

finally ready to receive it. Give me the window
lightning-split, the doors that won't close,

the linoleum curled at the kitchen baseboard,
the frayed silk patch worn couch. My mother's

childhood marbles sunk in the backyard sod,
Grandad's spiderwebbed toolbox, the note in

Grammy's handwriting swept in a draft from
where it slept for 30 years under the hall cabinet.

I can't have these without the others. Now
when I open a book and catch the flash of one

of your disciples, O Lady, I close it again, oh
so gently, and put it back upon the shelf.

Acknowledgements

Thanks to the editors who first published these poems:

"April Fool," *Crab Creek Review*, Fall 2015

"Asase Yaa Pins Her Clothing on the Line" (as "September Clothesline"), *The Commonline Journal*, September 2012

"As I Comb Lice from My Daughters' Hair," *Willow Springs*, Spring 2015

"As Soon As I Get Them," *Menacing Hedge*, Fall 2018

"Audubon's Birds of America, First Edition," *Grist*, Fall 2019

"The Blue Whale," Sue Boynton winning poems chapbook, 2018

"The Body Gifters," *Menacing Hedge*, Spring 2014

"The Bug Man Says," *Nimrod International Journal*, Spring 2017

"Distributary" *The Literary Review*, Summer 2018

"The Ex-Lovers," *Natural Bridge* No.35, Spring 2016

"The Fates Hang Wallpaper," *Clover, A Literary Rag*, Summer 2014

"Girls in Doorways and Other Phenomena," *Crab Creek Review*, Spring 2020

"Golden Lion Tamarin," *Spoon River Poetry Review*, Winter 2019

"Her Reduction," *Adelaide*, December 2016

"Homestead," *The Literary Review*, Summer 2018

"House of My Mother," *Poetry Northwest*, Summer 2020

"In the Side Yard," *Kahini Magazine*, June 2016

"Jackie," *Natural Bridge* No.35, Spring 2016; *The Lascaux Poetry Prize* anthology, 2018

"Little House," *Menacing Hedge*, Fall 2018

"Medea Does the Laundry," *Floating Bridge Review #7*, 2014

"Medusa Washes the Windows," *Wallpaper Magazine*, May 2018

"Mortgage," *Cincinnati Review*, May 2017

"Nocturne," *Adelaide*, December 2016

"One Step Forward, Two Steps Back," *Menacing Hedge*, Spring 2014

"Only One," *Qu Literary Magazine*, Winter 2017

"Our Lady of the Silverfish," *Psaltery & Lyre*, December 2019

"The Poisoning," *Clover, A Literary Rag*, Summer 2015

"Pluck," *Stirring: A Literary Collection*, May 2015

"Reflection in the Window at the Redlight," *Adelaide*, December 2016

"Rule of Three," *Nimrod International Journal*, Spring 2017

"The Sirens Take Out the Trash," *Sweet Tree Review*, Fall 2018

"Shoal," *Valparaiso Poetry Review*, Spring/Summer 2017
"Something Shining Up," *Psaltery & Lyre*, April 2017

"Spring, As Directed by Alfred Hitchcock," *Glassworks*, Spring 2016

"The Valkyries Clear the Table," *Psaltery & Lyre*, May 2017

"What If" as "Infinities," *Clover, A Literary Rag*, Fall/Winter 2014

"What's Left," *Split Rock Review*, Spring 2016

"What the Eclipse Taught Me," *Pittsburgh Poetry Review*, Spring 2018

Special thanks to Floating Bridge Press for publishing the chapbook *Endangered [Animal]*, in which these poems appeared: "The Blue Whale," "Audubon's *Birds of America*, First Edition," "Golden Lion Tamarin," "The Timber Wolf," "Magpie," and "The Hippopotamus".

My heart is full of gratitude for those who helped this book along the way, whether as readers or encouragers: Taneum Bambrick, Bruce Beasley, Dee Dee Chapman, Amy Guerra, Joshua Hilderbrand, Amorak Huey, Keetje Kuipers, Jessica Lee, Kelly Magee, Rachel Mehl, Brenda Miller, Hannah Newman, Dayna Patterson, Rena Priest, Laura Read, Eli Vignali, Emily Waters Shearer, Kami Westhoff, Steve Williamson, Jan Williamson, Melanie Wills, and Maya Jewell Zeller.

Thank you as well to Summer and everyone at Unsolicited Press for giving these poems a wonderful home.

Lastly, thank you to Josh, Naomia, Giorgi, Scarlett, and Aidan, for constantly teaching me new ways to love.

About the Author

Elizabeth Vignali is the author of *Object Permanence* (Finishing Line Press 2015) and *Endangered [Animal]* (Floating Bridge Press 2019), and coauthor of *Your Body A Bullet* (Unsolicted Press 2018). Her work has appeared in *Willow Springs*, *Cincinnati Review*, *Mid-American Review*, *Tinderbox*, *The Literary Review*, and others. She lives in the Pacific Northwest, where she works as an optician, coproduces the Bellingham Kitchen Session reading series, and serves as poetry editor of *Sweet Tree Review*.

ABOUT THE PRESS

Unsolicited Press is a small publisher in Portland, Oregon. The team is made up of incredible volunteers that seek to produce the highest quality poetry, fiction, and nonfiction. Follow the press on Twitter (@unsolicitedP), Instagram (@unsolicitedpress). Learn more at unsolicitedpress.com